SUPER QUESTION MARK SAVES THE DAY!

By Nadia Higgins • Illustrated by Mernie Gallagher-Cole

The Child's World®

Published by The Child's World®
1980 Lookout Drive • Mankato, MN 56003-1705
800-599-READ • www.childsworld.com

Acknowledgments
The Child's World®: Mary Berendes, Publishing Director
The Design Lab: Design and production
Red Line Editorial: Editorial direction

Design elements: Billyfoto/Dreamstime;
Dan Ionut Popescu/Dreamstime

ISBN 9781614732716
LCCN 2012932876

Printed in the United States of America
Mankato, MN
July 2012
PA02117

About the Author: Nadia Higgins is a children's book author based in Minneapolis, Minnesota. Nadia has been a punctuation fan since the age of five, when she first wrote "Happy Birthday!" on a homemade card. "I love punctuation because it is both orderly and expressive," Nadia says. Her dream is to visit Punctuation Junction someday.

About the Illustrator: Mernie Gallagher-Cole is a freelance children's book illustrator living outside of Philadelphia. She has illustrated many children's books. Mernie enjoys punctuation marks so much that she uses a hyphen in her last name!

The question marks of Punctuation Junction were always full of questions. But today was even more curious. Super Question Mark had called them all to a meeting at her superhero headquarters.

"As you know," she began, "tomorrow is April Fools' Day. It is our most important holiday. And I have come up with a wonderful prank. It is so unusual, interesting, suspicious, confusing, and wondrous. It will bring about more questions than ever!"

"Any questions?" Super Question Mark asked. The question marks used all six question words to hammer out the plan.

The questions went well into the night. But the question marks were too excited to be tired the next morning. Everyone arrived on time to the special spot.

Everyone knew where to go. Super Question Mark gave the instructions. "We'll hide and they will ask lots of questions," she said. "Then we'll jump out and yell surprise." They took their places . . . and they tried to stay still.

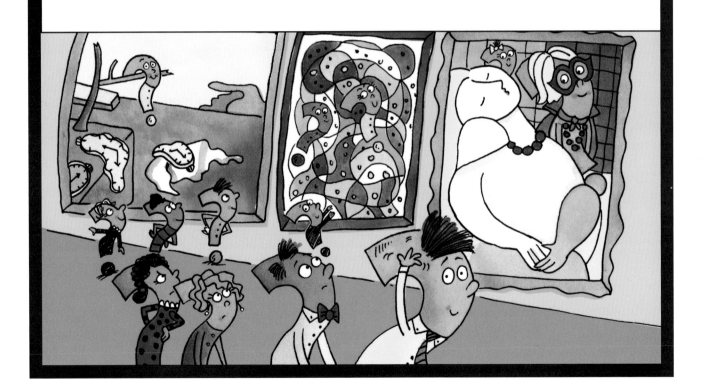

At last, the art lovers arrived.

"This painting!" Pam yelled. "I want to know everything about it!"

"I am so strangely interested in this splash of color," added Annie.

"I am bursting with questions about that green arm," said Emma.

"I feel awed, interested, captivated . . ." Karen murmured dreamily.

The plan was going great . . .

. . . except for one thing. With all the question marks hidden, nobody could ask any questions.

"I'm speechless with wonder," Pam said.

"My brain is exploding!" Annie cried.

"Call 9-1-1!" Emma screamed. "I'm dying of curiosity!"

Karen just fainted.

"Oh no!" said Super Question Mark. She had not counted on this. "Come out, question marks!" she called out as she leapt from her own painting. But then . . . *splat!* She snapped back flat against the canvas.

The other question marks squirmed, twitched, and yanked. It was no use. They were stuck.

This certainly was a job for a superhero.

Super Question Mark used her all of her super strength to break free from her painting. She helped Baby Q break free, too.

Then, with the power of *what*, the force of *when*, a burst of *who*, and some bolts of *where*, *why*, and *how*, she and Baby Q freed the question marks from their art prisons.

"What was I thinking? What went wrong? What if we had been stuck in there forever?" Super Question Mark started to go limp.

"It's all okay. You saved the day!" Pam the period hugged the superhero.

And what a day it was! All the punctuation marks agreed. It had been unusual, interesting, suspicious, confusing, and wondrous. Nobody could remember a day with more or better questions.

PUNCTUATION FUN

Quinn the quotation mark is writing an article for the *Punctuation Daily Messenger* about April Fools' Day at the museum. Super Question Mark has agreed to meet him for an interview. He will have 30 minutes to ask her questions for his story. Quinn is working on a list of questions to ask. He will need at least ten questions. Can you help him finish his list?

1. Where did you get the idea for your prank?

2. Did all the question marks think it was a good idea?

3. What painting did you hide inside?

4.

5.

6.

7.

8.

9.

10.

DO NOT WRITE IN THE BOOK!

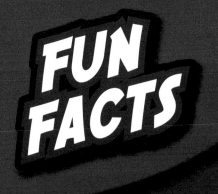

FUN FACTS

¿Why Not?

In Spanish, question marks are used at both the beginning and end of a question. The first question mark is upside down. The second one is normal. So, in Spanish, Baby Q says *¿Por qué?* That means "Why?" in English.

¿ yhW

In English, we read from left to right. Arabic speakers read from right to left. Everything is turned around—including question marks. In Arabic, a question mark looks like this: ¿

Instant Question

You can turn a sentence into a question. You just need to add a question mark at the end. We have all done it: *You are serious? I'm supposed to do that? You heard me?* In these cases, the question mark is very important. Think about how different these sentences would be with periods at the end.

Twenty Questions

Next time you are bored in the car, try playing the game Twenty Questions. One person thinks of something, but does not say his or her idea out loud. The "something" can be anything in the world: celery, a pet gerbil, a favorite movie, or a teacher. The other people have to guess what it is by asking questions. There is a catch, though. They can only ask questions that have "yes" or "no" answers. Sample questions could be: Is it living? Is it bigger than a car? Is it something you can touch? The guessers get 20 tries to find out.